Cornerstones of Freedom

The Story of

Live Aid

Susan Maloney Clinton

CHILDRENS PRESS®

CHICAGO

Library of Congress Cataloging-in-Publication Data

Clinton, Susan.
  Live Aid / by Susan Clinton.
    p. cm. — (Cornerstones of freedom)
  Summary: Describes the efforts of rock musician Bob
Geldof to organize the Live Aid concert to raise money
for famine victims in Ethiopia.
  ISBN 0-516-06665-X
  1. Live Aid (Fund raising enterprise)—Juvenile
literature. 2. Rock music—1981-1990—History and
criticism. 3. Geldof, Bob, 1954-   Juvenile literature.
4. Famines—Ethiopia—Juvenile literature. [1. Live Aid
(Fund raising enterprise) 2. Geldof, Bob, 1954-
3. Musicians. 4. Rock music—Biography.] I. Title.
II. Series.
ML3534.C6 1993
781.66′078421—dc20   92-33423
                                        CIP
                                     AC MN

Bob Geldof was a star. He sang with a rock group called the Boomtown Rats. Their biggest hit was a song called "I Don't Like Mondays." Bob Geldof had sung this song in front of a live audience hundreds of times before. He and the Boomtown Rats had performed in nightclubs, concert halls, and outdoor arenas. They had played all over England, Ireland, and the United States; they had given concerts in India, Germany, Finland, Thailand, Israel, and Japan. But they had never sung for a crowd this huge.

In front of Geldof, seventy-two thousand faces filled London's Wembley Stadium. Television

The crowd at Wembley Stadium on July 13, 1985

Ethiopian refugees living in temporary huts on the parched desert (above) and heading toward a relief camp (opposite page)

crews had their cameras focused on him. Geldof knew that beyond the thousands in the stadium, millions of people in 152 countries around the world were watching him on television. No concert had ever reached this many people before. But Bob Geldof wasn't playing in this concert for fame or for money or for fun; he was playing to save lives. It was July 13, 1985. This was the Live Aid concert.

A continent away, in the African nation of Ethiopia, 22 million people were starving. Seventeen years of low rainfall had parched crops, dried up wells, starved animals, and forced thousands of families to abandon their farms in search of food. These people could do nothing

David Bowie, George Michael, and Elton John at Live Aid in London

Fans at Wembley

now but wait for help. Bob Geldof was determined to help them.

His idea was to throw the biggest fund-raiser the world had ever seen: a huge rock concert with more than fifty of the world's greatest bands playing sixteen hours of music for the world's biggest audience. He named the concert "Live Aid"—*live* performances to *aid* starving people.

It took months of work and worry to organize Live Aid, but all the work paid off. The audience was enthusiastic and the music was great. The London crowd was treated to an unbelievable lineup of rock stars performing their greatest hits. David Bowie, Elton John, Elvis Costello, U2,

Bob Dylan, Keith Richards, and Madonna at Live Aid in Philadelphia

The Who, and former Beatle Paul McCartney all had a turn on stage.

But the London concert was only half of Live Aid. Across the ocean, in the United States, a crowd of ninety thousand filled JFK Stadium in Philadelphia to hear thirty-nine acts ranging from Madonna to the Beach Boys; from the rap group Run D.M.C. to folksinger Joan Baez. One musician, Phil Collins, managed to play in both concerts. After he performed with Sting in London, he boarded the Concorde, the fastest transatlantic passenger plane in the world. He reached Philadelphia in time to play drums onstage with the band Led Zeppelin.

Rick Springfield in Philadelphia

The two concerts were linked by satellite so that each audience could watch the other concert on huge TV monitors. When a group was performing on the London stage, the Philadelphia concert paused, and vice-versa. Geldof hoped to contrast the advanced technology of satellites and supersonic jets with the bare poverty of a country like Ethiopia. As he explained to a reporter, "To me this is not a pop concert, to me it is not a TV show, to me it is simply a means of keeping people alive." Live Aid succeeded beyond even Geldof's hopes; it was seen by 1.5 billion people, and raised over $100 million.

The audience at each concert could watch the other concert on huge TV screens.

Ethiopia is a rugged, mountainous country in northeast Africa.

It had been a TV broadcast that started it all,
back in the winter of 1984. British television had
aired a news story about the terrible famine in
northern Africa. *Famine* means there is no food.
Most people in England were shocked to find out
about the famine. They had not heard anything
about it before, yet thousands of Ethiopians—
men, women, and many, many children—had
already died. How could this happen? Why was
there no food? And why hadn't anyone outside
Ethiopia known about it until now?

Ethiopia is a large country in northeast Africa.
Its mountainous terrain is gouged by steep
valleys and deep ravines. This makes travel

An Ethiopian village

difficult; there are very few paved roads in
Ethiopia. In the country's desert regions, daily
temperatures can reach up to 120 degrees.

Most Ethiopians are subsistence farmers. This
means that they raise just enough to feed their
own families. It is a simple but hard way of life.
Children as well as adults help tend crops and
animals, carry water from wells, and gather
wood for cooking fires. Most of Ethiopia's
farmers live about half a day's walk from any
road. Many children cannot get to a school.
There are no stores in the rural areas; people
trade with their neighbors for the things they
need, so they don't have much use for money.

For about seventeen years, Ethiopia had been
suffering from a drought. This means that there

was very little rain. Wells and streams dried up. Crops could not grow in the dry, parched soil. Without roots to hold it, the soil simply blew away. Year by year, farmland was turning into useless desert.

Because the crops wouldn't grow, people were forced to eat the seeds they had saved for the next year's planting. And when those were gone, they had nothing. Nothing to grow, nothing to sell, nowhere to buy food, and no money to buy it. Thousands of Ethiopians made their way to relief camps, where agencies such as the Red Cross gave out free food. But when they arrived, these people were already starving, and many

Victims of the famine making their way to a relief camp

Many of those who reached the relief camps were already too weakened by starvation and disease to be helped.

were ill. The camps were crowded, with no running water, no bathrooms, sometimes not even shade from the hot sun. In these crowded and dirty conditions, disease spread easily. Relief agencies did not have enough food or medicine to help all the people who needed it.

Neither did the Ethiopian government. For one thing, the government was busy fighting wars. Ethiopia was waging a long war with the nearby nation of Somalia to see who would control the Ogaden desert area in eastern Ethiopia. The people in the northern Ethiopian provinces of

Eritrea and Tigray were also fighting for their independence. The war with Eritrea was particularly fierce. It had been going on for twenty-two years—ever since Eritrea had been joined to Ethiopia in 1962. When famine hit Eritrea and Tigray, the Ethiopian government did not want to help.

The leader of Ethiopia, Mengistu Haile Mariam, was afraid that if he asked for help from other countries, especially the United States, it would give them power to make changes in Ethiopia. When Mengistu came to power, in 1974, he made some good changes. For example, he gave poor families more land, and made people move into villages so they could have schools and markets. But he made these changes in a violent way, by killing people who disagreed with him. The government of the United States had always opposed his government. When the famine hit, the Ethiopian government did not want the world, especially the United States, to know how bad things were. Other countries might then blame Ethiopia's government for the disaster. Taking outside help would be admitting failure. By the time news of the famine reached the rest of the world, the Ethiopian people were in terrible need.

As a child and young man, Bob Geldof had never felt that he fit in. He grew up in Dublin, Ireland, very much on his own. His mother had

Somali rebels involved in the war over the Ogaden

Bob Geldof as a teenager

died suddenly when he was six years old. His father, a traveling salesman, was away during the week. Most evenings, Bob came home to an empty house, made himself something to eat, and spent the evenings alone. Although he was bright, he did not take much interest in school. He went to a very strict school where he was often punished with beatings. This only made him feel more rebellious. He tested every rule, especially those about wearing a tie and short hair. He was a scruffy teenager; tall, thin, and lanky with unruly brown hair and a full mouth. Some kids teased him, calling him Liver Lips. The teasing stopped after Rolling Stones singer Mick Jagger made full lips fashionable!

At seventeen, Bob left school and Ireland. He traveled about, taking a variety of jobs. He built roads in England, taught English in Spain, and wrote about music for a small newspaper in Vancouver, Canada. In 1975, he returned to Ireland with the plan of starting his own newspaper. But along the way, just for fun, he and his friends formed the Boomtown Rats. Bob was the band's songwriter and lead singer. Within a few years, the Rats went from being an unknown Irish rock band to being rock stars. Their concerts were jammed with fans. They had a string of hit songs. Finally, Bob Geldof had the freedom to say what he felt. He loved performing with the band; he sang all out. Fans loved him

Geldof singing as one of the Boomtown Rats

Bob Geldof's band, the Boomtown Rats, became very successful in the late 1970s.

and started wearing the big, black-and-white checked jackets that he wore.

In the late 1970s, the Boomtown Rats were a great success. By 1984, however, the band's popularity was fading. The Rats were working on a new album. Geldof was excited about it, but he couldn't get anyone else in the music industry to show much interest. He was afraid that after all their work, the new album would not sell. One night, he came home tired and discouraged. He sat down to watch the news on television, and what he saw changed his life.

He saw a camp in Ethiopia where, out of ten thousand starving people, there was enough food for only a few hundred. Geldof recalled, "There was this woman who had to pick three hundred people that she could feed. . . . The ones who hadn't been picked stood behind the waist-high wall and looked at them, without any rancor or envy but with intense dignity. That waist-high wall was the difference between life and death. And I remember seeing one child just put her head against the wall, the flies buzzing around her eyes. That's what made me do it. That one image is what made me do the whole thing."

The next day, Bob Geldof started calling Britain's biggest pop stars. His idea was to get a huge group of rock stars together to record a song. All the money made from the song would be used for famine relief in Africa. This supergroup took the name "Band Aid." The name had a double meaning. The group was indeed a band coming to the aid of people in need. But the famine problem was so severe that no matter how much money was raised, it would not be enough to help everyone—the effort was like putting a Band-Aid on a big wound. Still, Bob Geldof felt he had to do something to help, and music was what he did best. He figured that many people would buy such a record, just to hear all their favorite performers singing together. With the help of his friend Midge Ure,

The British rock stars who came together to form "Band Aid" in 1984

Geldof quickly wrote the song "Do They Know It's Christmas?" He lined up a studio to record it for free, and the performers agreed to sing for free. The record came out in time for Christmas 1984. Geldof's idea worked. Sales of the Band Aid record raised $11 million for famine relief.

Shortly after the Band Aid record came out, American musicians borrowed the idea and formed their own supergroup: USA for Africa. Together, they recorded a song written by Michael Jackson and Lionel Richie: "We Are the World." Bob Geldof was invited to the recording session. By this time, he had a new idea—a really big idea.

On April 18, 1985, Bob Geldof met with England's biggest pop-music promoter, Harvey Goldsmith. Promoters make bands famous by arranging concerts and news coverage. Geldof knew he would need help to pull off an event as big as the one he had in mind. He explained: if all the stars could come together for a record, why not for a concert—a huge, double concert, half in England, half in the United States? If a record could raise $11 million, a concert should be able to bring in four times as much!

Goldsmith liked the idea. He immediately began to think about the stage, the sound system, the lights, the equipment. Another big promoter who was at the meeting, Maurice Jones, agreed to work on selling tickets, producing posters, and getting publicity. They would try to get everything for free—the performers, the stage crews, the stadiums, the artwork—everything. They all agreed it could work. Then Geldof added one more thing. He wanted the two shows—the one in England and the one in America—to be linked by television satellite so that the audiences in both stadiums would see both concerts. "What?" said Goldsmith. Geldof talked him into it.

Then Geldof added one more thing. He wanted to have fifty bands. "Fifty?" Goldsmith shouted in disbelief. Geldof explained: the more big acts, the better. With fifty acts, each band would have about fifteen minutes—enough time to play only

A chart showing how Live Aid would be set up

their greatest hits. This would keep the audience from getting bored.

"That's impossible!" said Goldsmith. "You could never get a band and their equipment on and off stage in fifteen minutes . . . unless you divide the stage . . ." They started making drawings. They came up with a stage that was a big circle split into three parts. It would revolve, showing one band at a time. While one band was playing up front, the band that had just played would be clearing off, and the next band to play would be setting up. It would work!

Then Geldof added one more thing. He wanted the TV broadcast to be a global telethon. Every once in a while, television stations would interrupt the concert to give out a telephone number. Viewers could call that number to pledge money. Thousands of telephone lines would be needed to take calls in countries all over the world.

Goldsmith sat back for a moment and considered everything that Geldof had said. "How?" he asked.

Geldof shrugged his shoulders.

"Why?" Goldsmith asked.

"Because people are dying, Harvey," Geldof answered.

Goldsmith agreed to help. They picked a day: July 13, 1985. That day was only fourteen weeks away.

For help with the TV broadcast, Geldof enlisted Mike Mitchell. Mitchell's company, Worldwide Sports and Entertainment, had arranged television coverage of the 1984 Summer Olympics. Mitchell estimated that what Geldof wanted would ordinarily take two years to set up. He had ten weeks. He began by making deals with TV networks to send camera crews to broadcast the concert. At the same time, he asked one hundred countries to pay for the broadcast.

Bob Geldof and Paul McCartney during Live Aid

Geldof now had to get major stars to sing for free. Some of them, like Mick Jagger, said yes right away. Some took more persuading. Former Beatle Paul McCartney had not performed publicly in eight years. Geldof talked to McCartney's friends and called his manager. He wrote letter upon letter. Finally, McCartney said yes. At first, singer Tina Turner turned Geldof down; she had another concert in Canada that same night. But later, she canceled her Canadian concert and showed up to sing a hard-driving, sizzling duet with Mick Jagger in Philadelphia.

Geldof persuaded American promoter Bill Graham to help produce the Philadelphia concert. Graham brought in more American performers. Some of the American stars Graham and Geldof wanted said no. Others went back and forth. Geldof kept calling, he kept asking, he kept arguing. Lionel Richie said no, no, no, right up to the day of the concert because he was in

Tina Turner and Mick Jagger at Live Aid in Philadelphia

London's Wembley Stadium (above) and JFK Stadium in Philadelphia (right) getting ready for Live Aid

the middle of recording an album. At the last minute, however, he showed up at the finale of the Philadelphia concert to sing "We Are the World." The list of stars kept growing—but so did the list of problems.

All these problems found their way to Geldof. All through his childhood, he had had to be self-reliant. He did not accept anyone's opinion without questioning it, and he loved a good argument. Only someone like Bob Geldof would have had the confidence, the courage, and the sheer stubbornness to put Live Aid together. One by one, he dealt with the problems that arose—sometimes with persuasion, sometimes with threats.

Some European countries wanted to broadcast the concert but did not want to set up a telethon. He told them, "no telethon, no show." They set up telethons. The company that sold food at the London stadium refused to donate its profits to Live Aid. Rather than let this one company make a profit on Live Aid, Geldof announced that all ticket holders should bring their own picnic baskets and refuse to buy stadium food.

The stage designers in the United States lost the plans and ended up with a two-part stage instead of a three-part stage. Then, three weeks before the concert, Geldof discovered that whereas all the stage technicians were working for free in England, the American crews all expected to be paid. It was too late to change their deals with the American unions. Luckily, Mike Mitchell had obtained enough money from television sponsors to cover the cost of the American crews. Now Geldof could truthfully say that all the money from ticket sales and telethon contributions would go to famine relief.

As the concert drew closer, Geldof spent some time every day talking to reporters. It was important to get lots of Live Aid news coverage. The publicity worked. All the tickets for Live Aid—at $35 to $50 each—were sold a few hours after they went on sale.

By the day of the concert, five camera crews had been set up in Philadelphia. They would

Bob Geldof with the Prince and Princess of Wales at the start of the London concert

receive the British broadcast from Wembley and beam the whole concert out to the world using 14 satellites. The American stage was ready, with its 75 miles of electric cable, 120 big amplifiers, and 1,500 lights. In England, 1,000 telethon lines were open to receive calls. Taped messages from such world figures as South African bishop Desmond Tutu, former United States president Jimmy Carter, and India's prime minister Rajiv Gandhi were ready to go on the air.

Saturday, July 13, dawned sunny and clear on both sides of the Atlantic. As Bob Geldof rode over to Wembley Stadium, people on the street waved and wished him good luck. At the stadium, he was surrounded by photographers as he escorted Charles and Diana, the Prince and Princess of Wales, to their seats. The crowd gave a huge welcoming cheer, and the first band, Status Quo, opened with "Rock All Around the World." Everything was going smoothly. One act followed another right on time. Every performer onstage could see a set of three lights. The green light meant "you're on," the yellow light meant "one minute to go," and the red light meant "time's up—get off now."

As the stadium heated up, security guards sprinkled water on the dancing crowd. Bob Geldof was everywhere—watching the

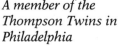

A member of the Thompson Twins in Philadelphia

Security guards help cool off the hot but happy crowd at Wembley.

Freddie Mercury of the rock group Queen performing at Wembley

performers, checking the TV coverage, making sure that the British telethon was bringing in calls. At one point, all one thousand telephone lines in England were jammed with calls. The American headquarters were getting 120,000 calls an hour. An aide called Geldof to the phone to talk personally with a man from Kuwait who wanted to pledge £1 million (about $3 million).

Money was coming in from countries all over the world.

At 10:00 P.M. in London, Paul McCartney and Pete Townshend of The Who lifted an exhausted but happy Bob Geldof up on their shoulders while the crowd cheered. Then, all the performers gathered onstage to sing the last song, "Do They Know It's Christmas?" Geldof later wrote, "There was a tremendous feeling of oneness on that stage. . . . everyone was singing. They had their arms around each other. . . . everyone was crying. Not the easy tears of showbiz but genuine emotion." In Philadelphia, the performers closed with an emotional chorus of "We Are the World." After sixteen hours of music, Live Aid was over. By the end of the day, Live Aid had raised about $40 million. But in the days and weeks to follow, the money kept coming in, until the total topped $100 million.

Bette Midler in Philadelphia

At the end of the London concert, Pete Townshend and Paul McCartney lifted Bob Geldof up on their shoulders while the crowd cheered.

In Philadelphia, the performers closed with an emotional chorus of "We Are the World."

Bob Geldof's job did not end with the concert. Geldof had asked a group of honest and concerned people to be Band Aid trustees. They had helped decide how to best spend the Band Aid money. They had also overseen the actual aid shipments. Like Geldof, all of them had worked without pay because they wanted every cent raised to go to Africa. As Geldof once said, it was "a great way not to make a living." Now he needed their help in deciding how to use the Live Aid money.

They spent millions immediately on short-term aid—things the people needed right away simply to stay alive. They bought 21,100 tons of food, 41 hospital tents with medical supplies, and 18 water trailers to provide pure drinking water in the relief camps. It cost millions more to transport these supplies to Africa by airlift, ship, and truck.

A book about the concert helped raise further funds.

Live Aid had made Bob Geldof more famous than ever. Reporters followed him everywhere. People called him "Saint Bob" and stuffed money in his pockets wherever he went. This scruffy Irish rock singer in crumpled jeans and lime-green sneakers had touched the conscience of the world. It didn't matter where people lived or what race they were or what their political beliefs were—they gave to Live Aid out of simple generosity.

With a group of reporters, he traveled across North Africa, drawing attention to countries suffering from the drought. Once he found out what was needed, Geldof went straight to the heads of state to make requests.

Geldof knew that the Ethiopian government did not want help from the United States, but would accept it if the money came through Live Aid. At a meeting with members of the U.S. Congress and officials of the United States Agency for International Development, Geldof asked if the United States would split the cost of

Some of the Live Aid money was used for long-term projects to help prevent famine in Africa, such as building irrigation systems.

bridging a river so that food could go across in trucks instead of canoes. The United States matched Live Aid, dollar for dollar.

Bob Geldof kept working hard because he knew that even though Live Aid had been a success, people would eventually lose interest in it. When that happened, Geldof's power to help, to influence governments, would be gone.

He worried about Africa's future. He and the trustees were careful to set aside about half of the money for long-term projects, such as drilling wells, building irrigation systems, and planting trees to hold the soil. As Geldof said to a reporter, "We have helped to keep people alive, and now we must give them a life. And so when the next drought comes, it will not be as disastrous."

Bob Geldof knew that all the Live Aid money would not be enough to protect Ethiopia or its neighbors from drought, war, disease, social upheaval, and poverty. Still, Geldof knew he had done as much as he could; he had helped keep millions of people alive. He also knew that, for a while, Live Aid had changed the way people felt about their fellow human beings. As he put it, "The legacy of [Live] Aid in Africa will be future generations allowed to live because of music and television and satellites and millions of people responding to the distant faint echo of their kinship with the rest of . . . Humanity."

After the concert, Geldof went to Africa to learn how the Live Aid money could best be put to use.

INDEX

PHOTO CREDITS

Cover, Rex USA Ltd.; 1, © Ken Regan/Camera 5; 2, 3, Rex USA Ltd.; 4, © Peter MacDiarmid/Rex USA Ltd.; 5, © Tony McGrath/Rex USA Ltd.; 6 (all 3 photos), Rex USA Ltd.; 7 (left), Wide World Photos; 7 (right, bottom), © Ken Regan/Camera 5; 8, Rex USA Ltd.; 9, 10, SuperStock; 11, 12 (both photos), © Peter MacDiarmid/Rex USA Ltd.; 13, AP/Wide World; 14 (top), Blackrock College; 14 (bottom), © Ken Regan/Camera 5; 15, © King Collection/Retna Pictures; 17 (top, bottom left), © Peter MacDonald/Rex USA Ltd.; 17 (bottom right), © C. Osborne/Valan Photos; 18, © Chip E./Retna Ltd.; 20, AP/Wide World; 21 (top), Rex USA Ltd.; 21 (bottom), © Ken Regan/Camera 5; 22 (left), Rex USA Ltd.; 22 (right), 24, AP/Wide World; 25 (top), © Ken Regan/Camera 5; 25 (bottom), Rex USA Ltd.; 26, © London Features Intl. USA; 27 (top), © Ken Regan/Camera 5; 27 (bottom), Reuters/Bettmann; 28, UPI/Bettmann; 29, Rex USA Ltd.; 30, © C. Osborne/Valan Photos; 31, © RDR Productions/Rex USA Ltd.

Picture Identifications:
Cover: The finale of the Live Aid concert in London
Page 1: Live Aid at JFK Stadium in Philadelphia
Page 2: Bob Geldof, the organizer of Live Aid

Project Editor: Shari Joffe
Designer: Karen Yops
Photo Editor: Jan Izzo
Cornerstones of Freedom Logo: David Cunningham

ABOUT THE AUTHOR

Susan Maloney Clinton holds a Ph.D. in English and is a part-time teacher of English literature at Northwestern University. Her articles have appeared in such publications as *Consumer's Digest*, *Family Style Magazine*, and the Chicago *Reader*. In addition, she has contributed biographical and historical articles to *Encyclopaedia Britannica* and *Compton's Encyclopedia*, and has written reader stories and other materials for a number of educational publishers. Ms. Clinton lives in Chicago with her husband, Pat, and their three children.

The author would like to thank the 1991-92 fourth-grade class at St. Gertrude School in Chicago, Illinois, for their adventurous spirits, their good hearts, and their clear thinking. She also thanks Sister Therese Waughon B.V.M. and Ms. Michelle Mohammadi for their gracious cooperation and support in this project.